SUPER CLIPART

FOR YOUTH WORKERS

CHECK OUT
THE SUPER COOL
TRACTS
INSIDE!

CARTOON ART,
BANNERS AND BORDERS
TO SUPERCHARGE YOUR
NEWSLETTERS, HANDBILLS
AND MAIL OUTS!!

SUPERPOWERED ART BY TOM FINLEY

FROM GOSPEL LIGHT

HOW TO MAKE CLEAN COPIES FROM THIS BOOK.

You may make copies of portions of this book with a clean conscience if:

→ you (or someone in your organization) are the original purchaser.

→ you are using the copies you make for a noncommercial purpose (such as teaching or promoting a ministry) within your church or organization.

→ you follow the instructions provided in this book.

However, it is illegal for you to make copies if:

→ you are using the material to promote, advertise or sell a product or service other than for ministry fundraising.

→ you are using the material in or on a product for sale.

→ you or your organization are **not** the original purchaser of this book.

By following these guidelines you help us keep our products affordable.

Thank you.

Gospel Light

EXECUTIVE STAFF
Mark Maddox, Publisher
Gary S. Greig, Ph.D., Senior Editor
Kyle Duncan, Managing Editor

INTRODUCTION

SUPER CLIP ART is your source for power-packed illustrations, mastheads and borders to super-energize your ministry's publications. And we've included a special treat: five spiritual growth tracts to photocopy and give to your kids.

Because we wanted the largest possible area for art on every page, this clip art book is not perforated. Tear out each page at the binding (especially when using the tracts) or use an X-acto knife to cut as close to the binding as necessary.

Now sit back, relax, eat your spinach and let your own creativity and the contents of this book unleash some terrific handbills, mail outs, and posters!

SUPER CONTENTS

Everything you need for a year's worth of mail outs, and more. Each section contains complete instructions and illustrations to guide you.

SUPER SIMPLE INSTRUCTIONS

Let your imagination do the walking! Just follow the step-by-step instructions and we guarantee that you'll produce super

mail outs
Bible study worksheets
posters
handbills
youth newsletters
overhead transparencies
T-shirt art

and an abundance of other high-powered show stoppers.

The Tools and Supplies You Need

- Rubber cement or glue stick
- Scissors
- White paper or card stock for paste-up
- Art from this book
- Optional: Typewriter
- Optional: Transfer (rub-on or peel-and-stick) letters and numbers.

Transfer letters are great for making special headlines. Buy them at any good art supply store. The manufacturers' catalogs have complete instructions.

Making the Masterpiece

1. Cut out the artwork and glue it down.

2. Use the headlines included with the art, or write your own.

3. Write or type your message on the paper (or on a separate sheet, which you can then glue down).

4. Run off as many copies as you need. That's it!

Some Super Samples:

SUPER CLIP ART SECTION

Here's all the clip art you need to promote your youth group's activities for at least a year—camps, Bible studies, games, sports, food, parties, music and more. Since the back of the clip art pages are blank you can cut them without ruining art on the reverse side.

13

SUPER CLIP TIP #1

MUCH OF THE ART IN THIS BOOK IS REPRODUCED IN MORE THAN ONE SIZE.

IF YOU HAVE ACCESS TO A COPIER THAT ENLARGES & REDUCES, TAKE ADVANTAGE OF IT!

LARGE FOOD THING!

18

20

CHURCH PICNIC!

SUPER CLIP TIP #2

TO GET AS MANY KIDS AS POSSIBLE TO SHOW UP FOR YOUR SPECIAL EVENTS, BE SURE TO FOLLOW UP YOUR CLIP ART PROMOTIONAL PIECES WITH A PHONE CALL THE NIGHT BEFORE THE EVENT.

SUPER CLIP TIP #3

AN ICE CHEST FULL OF ICE
WATER CAN MAKE A BIG
SPLASH IN SUNDAY SCHOOL!
PUT BIBLE QUESTIONS IN PLASTIC
BAGGIES WEIGHTED TO SINK.
KIDS GET THEM WITH BARE FEET.

THE ULTIMATE Challenge!

24

GIANT CONCERT...

30

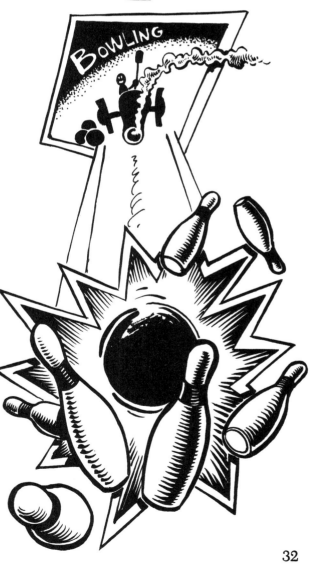

ICE HOCKEY

MINIATURE Golf

PRO SHOP GOLF!

It's Winter!

THE SKIS...THE TREES...THE BREEZE...THE **FREEZE**...

47

Winter

SNOW EXPERIMENT

CROSS COUNTRY

THE SKIS...THE TREES...THE BREEZE...THE FREEZE...

49

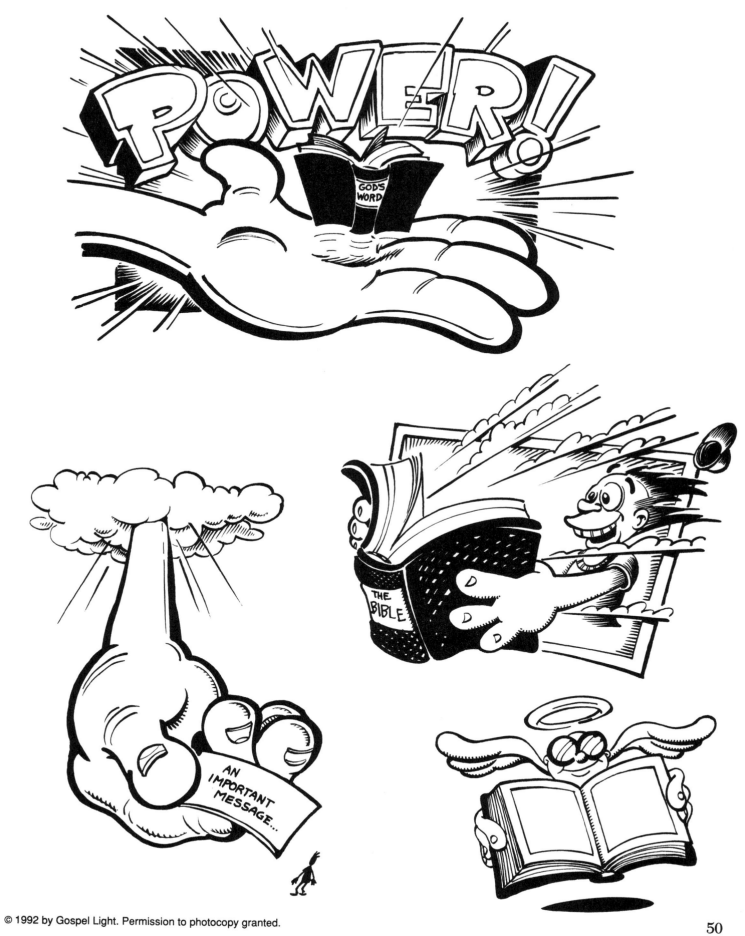

55

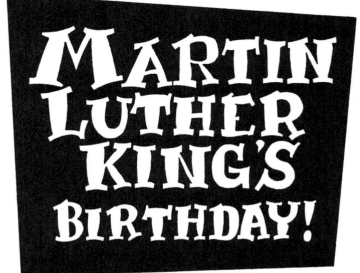

HAPPY NEW YEAR!

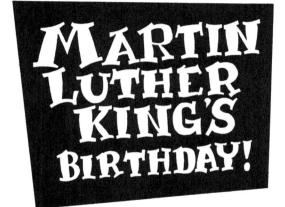

HI! A LOT OF US GOT TOGETHER AND THOUGHT WE'D COME UP WITH A **BRAND NEW YEAR!** BUT WE NEED YOUR HELP!

YEAH! YOU SEE, WE CAN'T FIGURE OUT **WHAT TO CALL IT.** A LOT OF NUMBERS, LIKE 1942 AND 1109 HAVE ALREADY BEEN TAKEN.

SO— WE'RE GONNA HAVE A **PARTY!** COME OUT AND HELP US PICK A NUMBER FOR THE NEW YEAR!

New Year's Party!

MARTIN LUTHER KING'S BIRTHDAY!

He's Risen!

CUPID WAS HERE

ACME PLUNGER CO.

EASTER

GET HERE ANY WAY YOU CAN...

GET HERE ANY WAY YOU CAN...

GET HERE ANY WAY YOU CAN...

TICK!
TICK!
TICK!

THE SECRET HANDSHAKE

SUPER MASTHEADS

Top off your great handbills with these terrific banners.

Every SUNDAY: Mondays: TUESDAYS: Each WEDNESDAY

events

June

July

August

HAVE YOU THOUGHT ABOUT SERVING GOD?

87

SUPER BORDERS

A good border can grab attention and quickly communicate the main theme of a promotional piece. Use the full size borders as paste-up sheets. Use the smaller borders to highlight special announcements.

If you've ever played Dart Wars, you'll appreciate our Dart War border. Haven't played? You must! Your youth group will beg you to play over and over again. Here's how to do it:

1. You need a dart gun and five "suction cup" darts for each player. Eye protection, such as dark glasses, is a must.

2. The game is played in the dark. If you play in your church building, be sure everyone understands what's off limits. Allow no one to move furniture or otherwise upset the facilities during play.

3. Divide the players into two teams. Send one team into the building (with the lights on) to find hiding spots. Turn off the lights and send in the other team.

4. When a player is hit with a dart he or she is out of the game and must go to a central lighted area. When a player is out of darts he or she is out (though players can use any darts they find or are given by "killed" teammates). After a set time limit, the team with the most surviving members wins.

Incredible

Scholarship FUND RAISER

$5 OFFICIAL SCHOLARSHIP FUND RAISING **$5**

BABY-SITTING CERTIFICATE

DISCIPLESHIP

GOD'S WORD

SERVICE *bulletin*

YOUR MISSION...

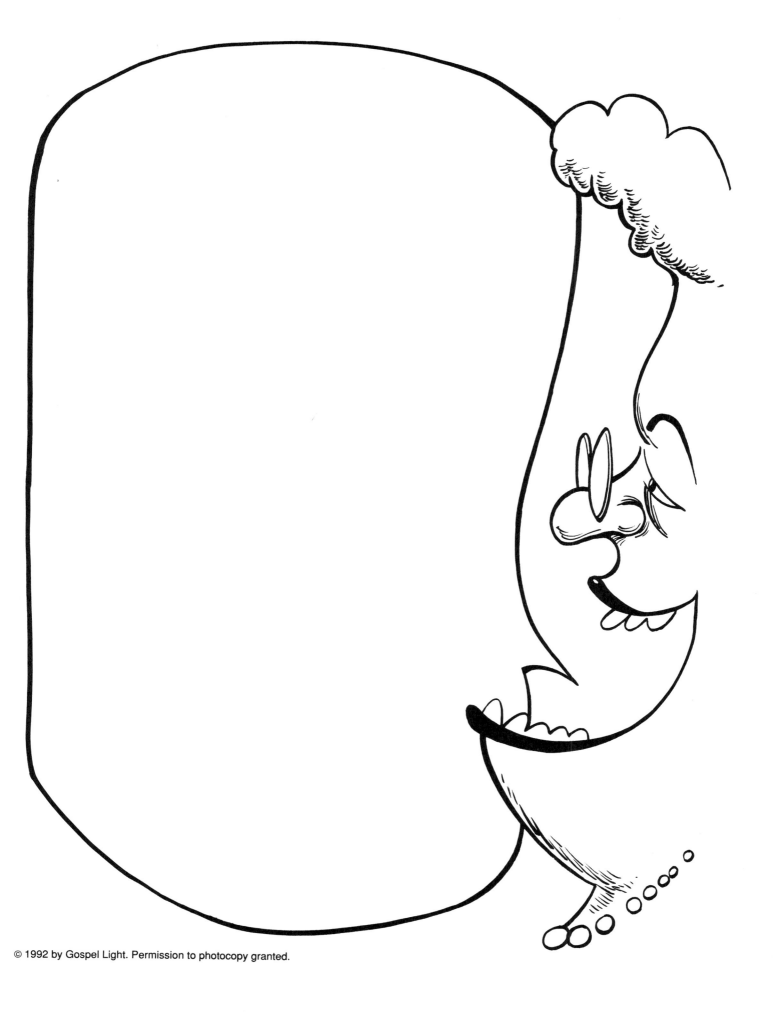

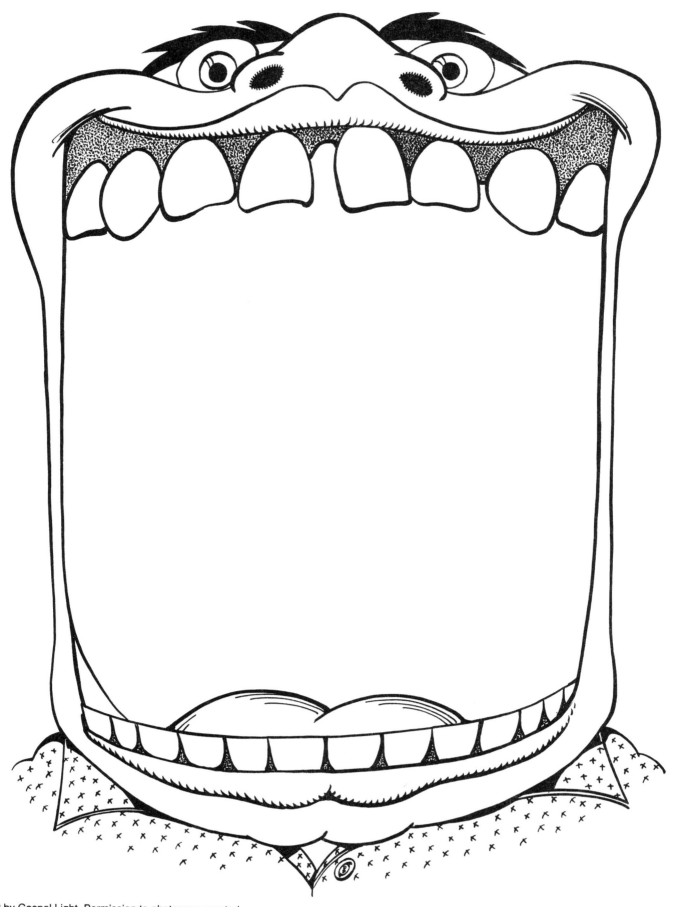

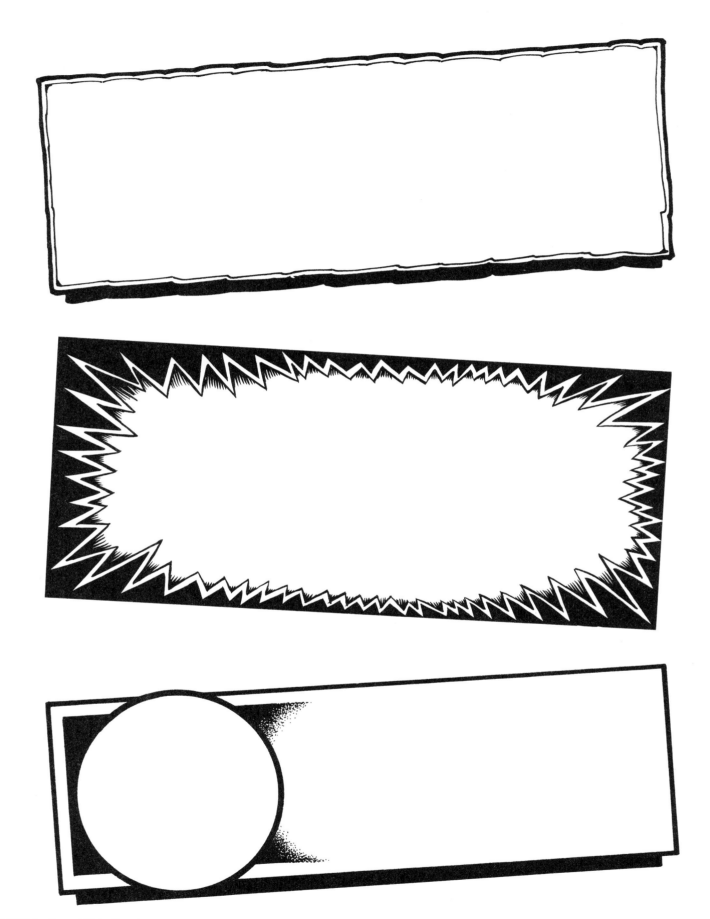

SPECIAL TREAT: REPRODUCIBLE TRACTS

Here are five gospel tracts that you can photocopy, fold and staple as shown below. Their subjects are salvation, taking problems to God, choosing to do good, cults and telling others about Christ. Three tracts are based on the Sleuth and Herschel Snodgrass—two cartoon characters originally developed for the Light Force Sunday School curriculum. All five can be given to newcomers or used in class as discussion starters. On the back of each is a space to put your church address and phone number.

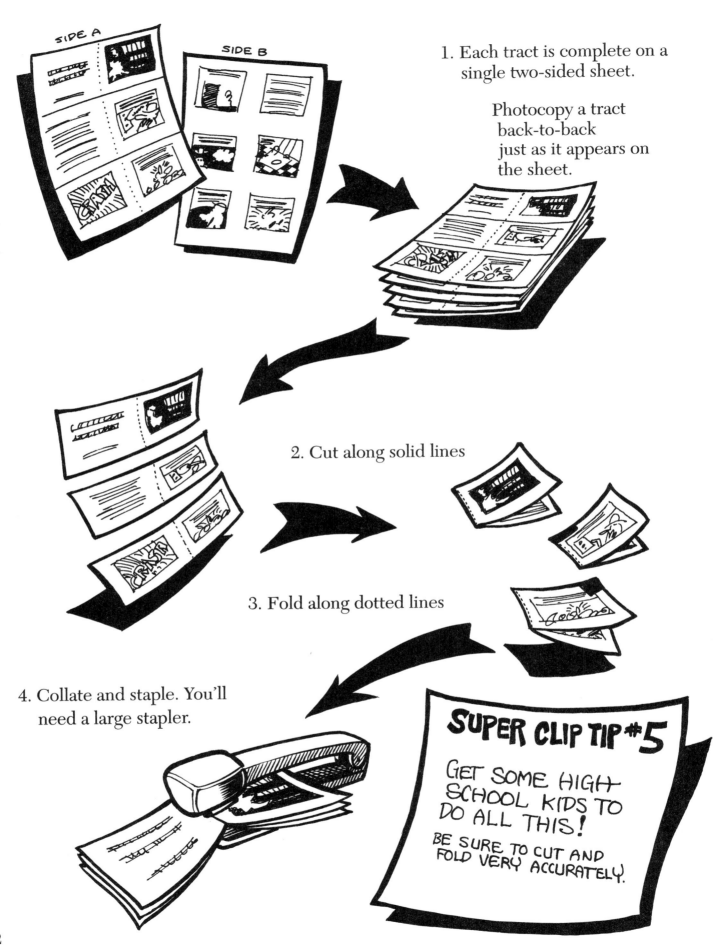

1. Each tract is complete on a single two-sided sheet.

   Photocopy a tract back-to-back just as it appears on the sheet.

2. Cut along solid lines

3. Fold along dotted lines

4. Collate and staple. You'll need a large stapler.

SUPER CLIP TIP #5

GET SOME HIGH SCHOOL KIDS TO DO ALL THIS!

BE SURE TO CUT AND FOLD VERY ACCURATELY.

Then talk to us. We'd be glad to tell you how to grow in Christ. Living for Jesus is fun! Join us.

⑫

It occurred to me that all I had to do was to have pushed the "Emergency Stop" button!

Here's something to think about—

Jesus claimed to be the only way to God:

"I am the way and the truth and the life. No one comes to the Father except through me" (John 14:6).

People may struggle to find ways to save themselves, but the truth is that Jesus is the one and only "Emergency Stop" button!

⑩

As you read on the previous page, Jesus claimed to be the **way** (to eternal life), the **truth** and the **life**. In John 8:31,32 Jesus said,

"If you hold to my teaching, you are really my disciples. Then you will know the truth, and the truth will set you free."

Would you like to be free? Free to enjoy life, free to be the person you'd like to be? Cling to the truth of Jesus! In prayer, ask Him to take charge of your life. Tell Him you want to belong to Him, then ask Him to teach you how to do that.

Got troubles? Give us a buzz:

HOW TO HANDLE YOUR PROBLEMS:
(Compare these to the list on the previous page)

1. First of all, come to Jesus like the woman did.
2. Recognize that you have a real need and only Jesus can handle it.
3. Have faith in Jesus; work on developing your faith.
4. Pray to the Lord about your troubles.
5. Place yourself close to the Lord, ready to be blessed when He answers. This usually means staying away from the things that cause your problems (if you get drunk at parties, don't go to parties). It also means talking to mature Christians God can use to help you.
6. Ask Him to help you with your problems!
7. Most of all—be sure Jesus is your Master! Not just someone you believe in, but someone you obey and serve.
8. If you do all of the above, Jesus will work with you to HANDLE YOUR PROBLEMS!

...OR THEY CAN BE A REAL BUMMER LIKE DRUGS, ALCOHOL, PARENT CONFLICTS, SCHOOL, ABUSE, ILLNESS, MONEY...

OK, ALREADY!

HOW CAN WE DEAL WITH ALL THIS?

THERE'S A STORY IN THE BIBLE. IT'S FOUND IN MATTHEW 15:22-28 — THE STORY OF A WOMAN WITH A PROBLEM TOO BIG FOR HER TO HANDLE!

SHE PASSED THE TEST! IN EFFECT, SHE SAID, "IF I'M A DOG, THEN YOU'RE MY MASTER"!

WOMAN, YOU HAVE GREAT FAITH! YOUR REQUEST IS GRANTED.

AND HER DAUGHTER WAS HEALED FROM THAT VERY HOUR.

PROBLEM SOLVED!

JESUS DID NOT ANSWER A WORD. SO HIS DISCIPLES CAME AND URGED HIM—

SEND HER AWAY, FOR SHE KEEPS CRYING OUT AFTER US.

YEH!

I WAS SENT ONLY TO THE LOST SHEEP OF ISRAEL.

AT THE TIME, IT WAS JESUS' MISSION TO WORK JUST WITH THE JEWS. THE LADY WASN'T JEWISH.

Try these on for size:

1. What are some of your problems that Jesus could help you solve?

2. How do most people who do not know Jesus deal with their problems? Would you rather do it their way or depend on God?

3. Why do you suppose God sometimes waits before handling a problem?

4. At times, God won't solve our problems as we hope, but in some other way. For example, a kid who can't walk may seek a cure—instead, God gives him a ministry to kids in the hospital. Why do you suppose God doesn't always do as we ask?

Let's check out this woman's PRINCIPLES FOR PROBLEM SOLVING:

1. She CAME TO JESUS. Jesus is strong enough to handle anything!
2. She CRIED OUT to Him. In her pain, she recognized her need and her inability to handle it.
3. She called Him "SON OF DAVID." She had faith FAITH in Jesus, calling Him the Messiah from God.
4. She TOLD HIM HER PROBLEM. Just like we do in prayer.
5. She KNELT BEFORE JESUS. She placed herself in a position to be touched and blessed by the Lord.
6. She ASKED THE LORD FOR HELP. Don't forget to ask!
7. She called Jesus her MASTER. She was a believer; Jesus was her Master!
8. Jesus responded: PROBLEM SOLVED!

For more information, give us a call!

⑫

There's no such thing as a "Good Cookie" or any other thing that will instantly make you a nice person. Being good is something you must decide to do yourself. That's why Peter gives us this advice:

"Whoever would love life and see good days must keep his tongue from evil and his lips from deceitful speech. He must turn from evil and do good; he must seek peace and pursue it. For the eyes of the Lord are on the righteous and his ears are attentive to their prayer, but the face of the Lord is against those who do evil" (1 Peter 3:10-12).

In other words, it's up to you to **choose** the right thing.

But how can you do the right thing? After all, we have tempers, we wake up grumpy, we say bad things, we gossip—we just don't seem able to always do the right thing.

⑩

Only a person who has been **supernaturally changed by God** could hope to become the good person He wants each of us to be. That's why we talk of conversion when we talk about becoming a Christian. To be converted means to be transformed by God from the old non-Christian person into a whole new being:

"Do not conform any longer to the pattern of this world, but be transformed by the renewing of your mind"
(Romans 12:2).

It is God who transforms us! Read your Bible, talk to Him in prayer, live for God. He'll change your life.